The Fab-YOU-list

*A Daily Discovery Guide
for Your Most FabYOUlous Life*

by

Melissa Venable

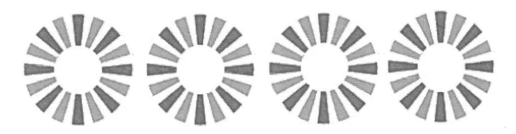

The Fab-YOU-list   Melissa Venable

Version 1.0 ~ 2018

Pubished by *FabYOUlous Life Publishing*

ISBN: 9781730766275

Copyright © 2018 by Melissa Venable

Discover other titles by Melissa Venable at *www.FabYOUlousLife.com*

Cover design by Danielle Raine

This book is a guided discovery journal and is not intended to serve as or take the place of professional counseling/therapy. Results may vary depending upon each individual reader's personal response to the journaling prompts. Any internet references contained within this book are current as of publication time, but the publisher cannot guarantee that a specific online reference will continue to be maintained.

All rights reserved, including the right of reproduction in whole or in part in any form.

For bulk ordering inquiries, please visit the contact tab at www.FabYOUlousLife.com

In Gratitude

Always and forever, thank you to Dave. You lovingly protect the parts of me that are vulnerable, while shining a light on the parts of me that are beautiful. Most importantly—you're the one person on the planet who knows *ALL* of those parts and yet, still loves me so magically.

To my Walker and Creighton. The very best parts of me are a direct result of loving you. Your mama will always love you more than all the stars in the sky.

To my bonus daughter, Becca. I love you. Plain and simple. You are a delight and a tremendous gift in my life.

To my mom and dad. Your girl's on fire. Thank you for always doing your part to fan the flame—while keeping an eye to make sure that she doesn't burn out. I love you.

To everyone who is tired of living the same day over and over again. This is your book and now is your time. You've got this.

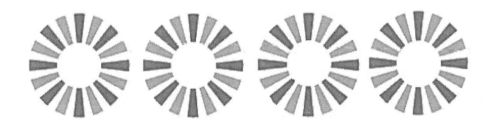

Introduction

There are so many other things that you could be doing with your time right now, so let me first just say a huge and heartfelt thank you for picking up this book and choosing to invest your time in this space.

As you are no doubt already aware, this isn't a normal book that you plop down with a cup of tea (or glass of wine) and just start reading. No, instead, this is a book that you *write*. It's a book that takes you on a yearlong journey back to yourself through a series of guided list-making exercises.

If you've read my first book, *Finding FabYOUlous: A 'Self-Help with Sass' Guide to Finding, Celebrating and Capitalizing on the FabYOUlousness that Makes You, YOU*, you already know how important it is to have a firm grasp on who you are and what makes you unique. *This* book is simply a tool that can help to make that self-knowing a bit easier (and more fun). These daily lists have been specifically selected to take you on a revealing journey of self-discovery in a gentle and nurturing way that facilitates personal growth.

Ideally, you'd start this process on the first day of a new year, January 1. However; that isn't necessary. You might also choose to begin this journey on your birthday or perhaps, the third Tuesday in March. When you start the journey isn't important—*completing* the journey is what matters.

To begin this journey, simply open the book and turn to the page with today's date at the top of it. If you are beginning on January 1, this will be page one, but if you are beginning on August 6, you'll begin on page 218. Be sure to start on the current date and don't worry about the pages that you've "missed". You haven't missed them—you'll circle back to them in the following year as you undertake this 365-day adventure. The lists follow a specific progression and are synced with seasons, months etc. Beginning on the current date, even if that isn't the start of the book, will ensure that you are aligned with the natural flow of this self-discovery process.

While I've never been a real stickler for rules, I do feel that it is important to offer a few guidelines as you start off on this exploration of self. These suggestions will simply ensure that you gain the most benefit from the time that you spend in these pages, and that your journey back to yourself is an enjoyable and enlightening one.

Guidelines for Making the Most of this Book

- Flip to the page with today's date at the top and begin there. I know that we've already covered this one, but it's important. Don't worry about the pages that you've missed—this is a 365 day exercise—you'll come back around to them.
- Select a time of day that works best for you to do your lists and then stick to it. Personally, I'm a night owl, so doing my lists at night is what works best for me. Many people prefer to do their lists in the morning as a part of their morning routine, while others make time during their lunch hour. It doesn't really matter when you choose to do the lists, as long as it is a time that works for you. The important thing is to pick your time and then stick with it. Consistency is the key to forming new habits

and we want this list making exercise to become a new self-care habit for you.

- Don't skip lists. Some lists will be easy to make while others may bring up emotions or memories that you'd rather not deal with. These uncomfortable feelings are all a part of the ongoing self-discovery process and an important part of your story. Don't worry—we won't dwell on difficult subjects, but it is important that these challenging emotions be acknowledged and honored for the lessons that they teach. Don't shy away from a list just because it makes you uneasy.
- Give yourself time to complete your lists. Some lists will be easy to complete while others will require more thought. Don't rush the process.
- Do your best. There may be some lists in this book for which you can come up with a hundred answers, while other lists will have you struggling to come up with two. That's normal and expected. The level of difficulty that a list presents offers just as much insight as do the answers. If you truly only have two answers for a list—let it be. That in itself, reveals a great deal about your inner workings.
- Make additional notes. On every page, there is a bit of space after the final entry. This is intentional. Use this space to jot any additional thoughts or feelings that you have regarding that day's list.
- Most importantly—HAVE FUN. If you find a list that you particularly like, share it with your family around the dinner table and ask for their answers. Let your mind wander to memories from childhood and dream big when making lists about the future. These lists are *your* lists. Have fun with them and let them open you up to new ideas and cherished memories.

In a year, you'll know more about yourself than you thought possible and be a wiser person for it.

Now—grab a pen, get comfy and let's get started with your first FabYOUlist...

Don't forget to follow the FAB
www.FabYOUlousLife.com

@FabYOUlousLife   @FabYOUlous_Life   @FabYOUlousLife   @FabYOUlousLife

 Self awareness is one of the rarest of human commodities ~Tony Robbins~

January 1

 List 10 things that you hope to accomplish this year...

1.

2.

3.

4.

5.

6.

7.

8.

9.

10.

January 2

 List 10 great things that happened this past year

1.

2.

3.

4.

5.

6.

7.

8.

9.

10.

January 3

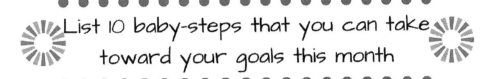

List 10 baby-steps that you can take toward your goals this month

1.

2.

3.

4.

5.

6.

7.

8.

9.

10.

January 4

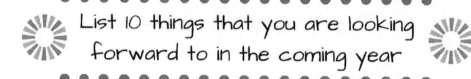
List 10 things that you are looking forward to in the coming year

1.

2.

3.

4.

5.

6.

7.

8.

9.

10.

January 5

 List your 10 most dominant personality traits

1.

2.

3.

4.

5.

6.

7.

8.

9.

10.

January 6

 List 10 things that you loved doing as a child

1.

2.

3.

4.

5.

6.

7.

8.

9.

10.

January 7

 List 10 things that you are looking forward to this week

1.

2.

3.

4.

5.

6.

7.

8.

9.

10.

January 8

List 10 things that you love about winter

1.

2.

3.

4.

5.

6.

7.

8.

9.

10.

January 9

 List 10 goals that you have for the next 90 days

1.

2.

3.

4.

5.

6.

7.

8.

9.

10.

January 10

 List 10 places that you would like to visit in your lifetime

1.

2.

3.

4.

5.

6.

7.

8.

9.

10.

January 11

 List 10 things that make you feel hopeful

1.

2.

3.

4.

5.

6.

7.

8.

9.

10.

January 12

 List 10 skills/talents that you admire in others

1.

2.

3.

4.

5.

6.

7.

8.

9.

10.

January 13

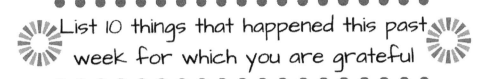
List 10 things that happened this past week for which you are grateful

1.

2.

3.

4.

5.

6.

7.

8.

9.

10.

January 14

 List 10 things that you are looking forward to this week

1.

2.

3.

4.

5.

6.

7.

8.

9.

10.

January 15

 List your 10 most deeply held beliefs

1.

2.

3.

4.

5.

6.

7.

8.

9.

10.

January 16

 List 10 contributions that you have already made to the world

1.

2.

3.

4.

5.

6.

7.

8.

9.

10.

January 17

 List 10 contributions that you still hope to make in the world

1.

2.

3.

4.

5.

6.

7.

8.

9.

10.

January 18

 List 10 things that make you feel strong

1.

2.

3.

4.

5.

6.

7.

8.

9.

10.

January 19

 List 10 things that make you feel vulnerable

1.

2.

3.

4.

5.

6.

7.

8.

9.

10.

January 20

List 10 things that happened this past week for which you are grateful

1.

2.

3.

4.

5.

6.

7.

8.

9.

10.

January 21

 List 10 things that you are looking forward to this week

1.

2.

3.

4.

5.

6.

7.

8.

9.

10.

January 22

List 10 personality/character traits that you admire in others

1.

2.

3.

4.

5.

6.

7.

8.

9.

10.

January 23

 List 10 things that have always been easy for you

1.

2.

3.

4.

5.

6.

7.

8.

9.

10.

January 24

List 10 things that you would most want to save if your house caught fire

1.

2.

3.

4.

5.

6.

7.

8.

9.

10.

January 25

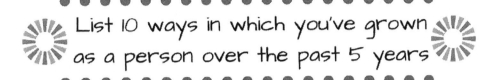

List 10 ways in which you've grown as a person over the past 5 years

1.

2.

3.

4.

5.

6.

7.

8.

9.

10.

January 26

 List 10 values that are absolute non-negotiables for you

1.

2.

3.

4.

5.

6.

7.

8.

9.

10.

January 27

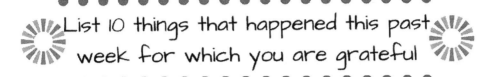
List 10 things that happened this past week for which you are grateful

1.

2.

3.

4.

5.

6.

7.

8.

9.

10.

January 28

List 10 things that you are looking forward to this week

1.

2.

3.

4.

5.

6.

7.

8.

9.

10.

January 29

 List the 10 greatest days of your life so far

1.

2.

3.

4.

5.

6.

7.

8.

9.

10.

January 30

 List 10 locations that have special meaning to you

1.

2.

3.

4.

5.

6.

7.

8.

9.

10.

January 31

 List 10 highlights of the past month

1.

2.

3.

4.

5.

6.

7.

8.

9.

10.

February 1

List 10 things that you are looking forward to this month

1.

2.

3.

4.

5.

6.

7.

8.

9.

10.

February 2

 List 10 adjectives that describe your best friend

1.

2.

3.

4.

5.

6.

7.

8.

9.

10.

February 3

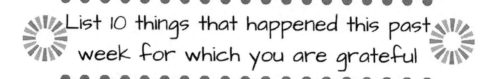
List 10 things that happened this past week for which you are grateful

1.

2.

3.

4.

5.

6.

7.

8.

9.

10.

February 4

 List 10 things that you are looking forward to this week

1.

2.

3.

4.

5.

6.

7.

8.

9.

10.

February 5

 List 10 books that you have enjoyed reading

1.

2.

3.

4.

5.

6.

7.

8.

9.

10.

February 6

List 10 items that are cluttering up your work/living space

1.

2.

3.

4.

5.

6.

7.

8.

9.

10.

February 7

 List your 10 favorite things about the nighttime

1.

2.

3.

4.

5.

6.

7.

8.

9.

10.

February 8

List your 10 favorite things about the daytime

1.

2.

3.

4.

5.

6.

7.

8.

9.

10.

February 9

List 10 things that you would change about the world, if you had the power

1.

2.

3.

4.

5.

6.

7.

8.

9.

10.

February 10

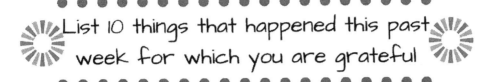
List 10 things that happened this past week for which you are grateful

1.

2.

3.

4.

5.

6.

7.

8.

9.

10.

February 11

List 10 things that you are looking forward to this week

1.

2.

3.

4.

5.

6.

7.

8.

9.

10.

February 12

 List 10 traits that your significant other must possess

1.

2.

3.

4.

5.

6.

7.

8.

9.

10.

February 13

List 10 ways that you enjoy expressing love for others

1.

2.

3.

4.

5.

6.

7.

8.

9.

10.

February 14

List 10 ways that you can express love for yourself

1.

2.

3.

4.

5.

6.

7.

8.

9.

10.

February 15

 List 10 things that make you feel loved and appreciated

1.

2.

3.

4.

5.

6.

7.

8.

9.

10.

February 16

 List 10 emotions that you have experienced so far this week

1.

2.

3.

4.

5.

6.

7.

8.

9.

10.

February 17

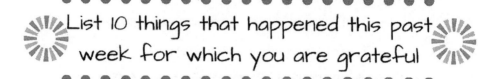
List 10 things that happened this past week for which you are grateful

1.

2.

3.

4.

5.

6.

7.

8.

9.

10.

February 18

 List 10 things that you are looking forward to this week

1.

2.

3.

4.

5.

6.

7.

8.

9.

10.

February 19

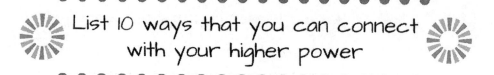

List 10 ways that you can connect with your higher power

1.

2.

3.

4.

5.

6.

7.

8.

9.

10.

February 20

 List 10 adjectives that describe your past 5 years

1.

2.

3.

4.

5.

6.

7.

8.

9.

10.

February 21

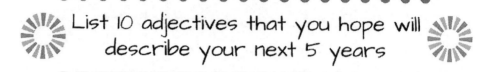

List 10 adjectives that you hope will describe your next 5 years

1.

2.

3.

4.

5.

6.

7.

8.

9.

10.

February 22

 List your 10 favorite daily activities

1.

2.

3.

4.

5.

6.

7.

8.

9.

10.

February 23

 List 10 sounds that you can hear right now

1.

2.

3.

4.

5.

6.

7.

8.

9.

10.

February 24

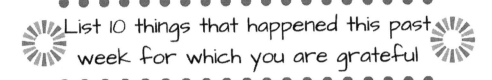
List 10 things that happened this past week for which you are grateful

1.

2.

3.

4.

5.

6.

7.

8.

9.

10.

February 25

List 10 things that you are looking forward to this week

1.

2.

3.

4.

5.

6.

7.

8.

9.

10.

February 26

 List 10 celebrities that you look up to

1.

2.

3.

4.

5.

6.

7.

8.

9.

10.

February 27

 List 10 "real people" that you look up to

1.

2.

3.

4.

5.

6.

7.

8.

9.

10.

February 28

 List 10 highlights of the past month

1.

2.

3.

4.

5.

6.

7.

8.

9.

10.

March 1

List 10 things that you are looking forward to this month

1.

2.

3.

4.

5.

6.

7.

8.

9.

10.

March 2

List 10 positive adjectives that you feel describe you

1.

2.

3.

4.

5.

6.

7.

8.

9.

10.

March 3

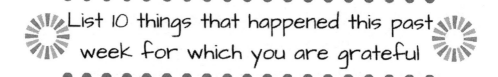
List 10 things that happened this past week for which you are grateful

1.

2.

3.

4.

5.

6.

7.

8.

9.

10.

March 4

 List 10 things that you are looking forward to this week

1.

2.

3.

4.

5.

6.

7.

8.

9.

10.

March 5

List 10 household chores that you hate doing

1.

2.

3.

4.

5.

6.

7.

8.

9.

10.

March 6

 List 10 household chores that you don't mind doing

1.

2.

3.

4.

5.

6.

7.

8.

9.

10.

March 7

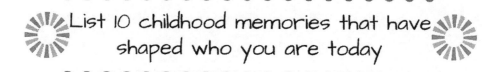

List 10 childhood memories that have shaped who you are today

1.

2.

3.

4.

5.

6.

7.

8.

9.

10.

March 8

 List 10 ways in which you sabotage your own success

1.

2.

3.

4.

5.

6.

7.

8.

9.

10.

March 9

 List 10 things that you love about your life right now

1.

2.

3.

4.

5.

6.

7.

8.

9.

10.

March 10

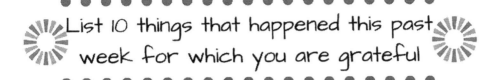
List 10 things that happened this past week for which you are grateful

1.

2.

3.

4.

5.

6.

7.

8.

9.

10.

March 11

 List 10 things that you are looking forward to this week

1.

2.

3.

4.

5.

6.

7.

8.

9.

10.

March 12

 List 10 attributes of your perfect day

1.

2.

3.

4.

5.

6.

7.

8.

9.

10.

March 13

 List your 10 favorite foods

1.

2.

3.

4.

5.

6.

7.

8.

9.

10.

March 14

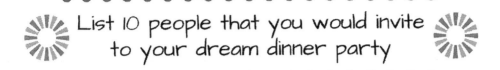

List 10 people that you would invite to your dream dinner party

1.

2.

3.

4.

5.

6.

7.

8.

9.

10.

March 15

 List 10 scents that you love

1.

2.

3.

4.

5.

6.

7.

8.

9.

10.

March 16

List 10 traits that you admire in the opposite sex

1.

2.

3.

4.

5.

6.

7.

8.

9.

10.

March 17

List 10 things that happened this past week for which you are grateful

1.

2.

3.

4.

5.

6.

7.

8.

9.

10.

March 18

 List 10 things that you are looking forward to this week

1.

2.

3.

4.

5.

6.

7.

8.

9.

10.

March 19

 List 10 physical activities that you enjoy

1.

2.

3.

4.

5.

6.

7.

8.

9.

10.

March 20

List 10 super powers (in order of preference) that you would like to have

1.

2.

3.

4.

5.

6.

7.

8.

9.

10.

March 21

 List 10 items that you currently have but don't use/want

1.

2.

3.

4.

5.

6.

7.

8.

9.

10.

March 22

 List 10 items that you currently have and use/want a great deal

1.

2.

3.

4.

5.

6.

7.

8.

9.

10.

March 23

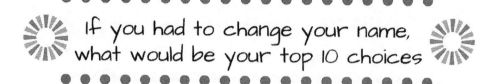

If you had to change your name, what would be your top 10 choices

1.

2.

3.

4.

5.

6.

7.

8.

9.

10.

March 24

List 10 things that happened this past week for which you are grateful

1.

2.

3.

4.

5.

6.

7.

8.

9.

10.

March 25

List 10 things that you are looking forward to this week

1.

2.

3.

4.

5.

6.

7.

8.

9.

10.

March 26

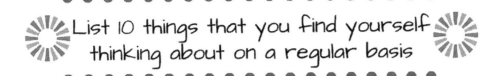
List 10 things that you find yourself thinking about on a regular basis

1.

2.

3.

4.

5.

6.

7.

8.

9.

10.

March 27

 List 10 things that make you shine

1.

2.

3.

4.

5.

6.

7.

8.

9.

10.

March 28

List 10 colors that have special meaning to you

1.

2.

3.

4.

5.

6.

7.

8.

9.

10.

March 29

 List 10 people whom you have positively influenced

1.

2.

3.

4.

5.

6.

7.

8.

9.

10.

March 30

List 10 characteristics that you consider to be attributes of success

1.

2.

3.

4.

5.

6.

7.

8.

9.

10.

March 31

 List 10 highlights of the past month

1.

2.

3.

4.

5.

6.

7.

8.

9.

10.

April 1

 List 10 things that you are looking forward to this week

1.

2.

3.

4.

5.

6.

7.

8.

9.

10.

April 2

 List 10 things that you are looking forward to this month

1.

2.

3.

4.

5.

6.

7.

8.

9.

10.

April 3

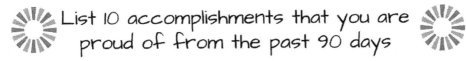 List 10 accomplishments that you are proud of from the past 90 days

1.

2.

3.

4.

5.

6.

7.

8.

9.

10.

April 4

 List 10 goals that you have for the next 90 days

1.

2.

3.

4.

5.

6.

7.

8.

9.

10.

April 5

 List your 10 biggest turn ons

1.

2.

3.

4.

5.

6.

7.

8.

9.

10.

April 6

List your 10 biggest turn offs

1.

2.

3.

4.

5.

6.

7.

8.

9.

10.

April 7

List 10 things that happened this past week for which you are grateful

1.

2.

3.

4.

5.

6.

7.

8.

9.

10.

April 8

 List 10 things that you are looking forward to this week

1.

2.

3.

4.

5.

6.

7.

8.

9.

10.

April 9

 List your 10 all-time favorite movies

1.

2.

3.

4.

5.

6.

7.

8.

9.

10.

April 10

 List 10 contradictory aspects of your personal nature

1.

2.

3.

4.

5.

6.

7.

8.

9.

10.

April 11

List 10 things that you would like to be known for

1.

2.

3.

4.

5.

6.

7.

8.

9.

10.

April 12

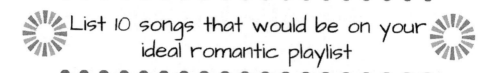
List 10 songs that would be on your ideal romantic playlist

1.

2.

3.

4.

5.

6.

7.

8.

9.

10.

April 13

 List 10 elements of your ideal vacation

1.

2.

3.

4.

5.

6.

7.

8.

9.

10.

April 14

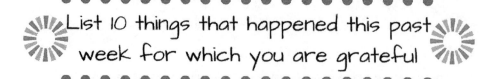
List 10 things that happened this past week for which you are grateful

1.

2.

3.

4.

5.

6.

7.

8.

9.

10.

April 15

List 10 things that you are looking forward to this week

1.

2.

3.

4.

5.

6.

7.

8.

9.

10.

April 16

 List 10 things that you love about spring

1.

2.

3.

4.

5.

6.

7.

8.

9.

10.

April 17

 List 10 pieces of advice that you would give to your younger self

1.

2.

3.

4.

5.

6.

7.

8.

9.

10.

April 18

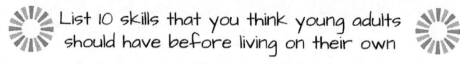

List 10 skills that you think young adults should have before living on their own

1.

2.

3.

4.

5.

6.

7.

8.

9.

10.

April 19

 List 10 ways that you connect with nature

1.

2.

3.

4.

5.

6.

7.

8.

9.

10.

April 20

List 10 activities that enjoy during your free time

1.

2.

3.

4.

5.

6.

7.

8.

9.

10.

April 21

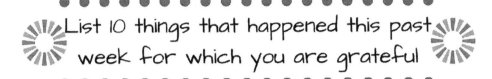
List 10 things that happened this past week for which you are grateful

1.

2.

3.

4.

5.

6.

7.

8.

9.

10.

April 22

 List 10 things that you are looking forward to this week

1.

2.

3.

4.

5.

6.

7.

8.

9.

10.

April 23

 List the 10 character traits that you most despise

1.

2.

3.

4.

5.

6.

7.

8.

9.

10.

April 24

List 10 doors that you have closed or bridges that you have burned

1.

2.

3.

4.

5.

6.

7.

8.

9.

10.

April 25

 List 10 things that keep you going when times are hard

1.

2.

3.

4.

5.

6.

7.

8.

9.

10.

April 26

 List 10 websites that you visit on a regular basis

1.

2.

3.

4.

5.

6.

7.

8.

9.

10.

April 27

 List your 10 dream jobs

1.

2.

3.

4.

5.

6.

7.

8.

9.

10.

April 28

List 10 things that happened this past week for which you are grateful

1.

2.

3.

4.

5.

6.

7.

8.

9.

10.

April 29

 List 10 things that you are looking forward to this week

1.

2.

3.

4.

5.

6.

7.

8.

9.

10.

April 30

List 10 highlights of the past month

1.

2.

3.

4.

5.

6.

7.

8.

9.

10.

May 1

 List 10 things that you are looking forward to this month

1.

2.

3.

4.

5.

6.

7.

8.

9.

10.

May 2

 List 10 self-care activities that help you to relax

1.

2.

3.

4.

5.

6.

7.

8.

9.

10.

May 3

List 10 items that have deep, sentimental meaning to you

1.

2.

3.

4.

5.

6.

7.

8.

9.

10.

May 4

 List 10 things that cause you to feel envious

1.

2.

3.

4.

5.

6.

7.

8.

9.

10.

May 5

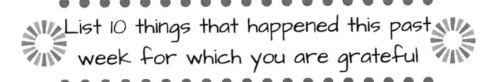
List 10 things that happened this past week for which you are grateful

1.

2.

3.

4.

5.

6.

7.

8.

9.

10.

May 6

 List 10 things that you are looking forward to this week

1.

2.

3.

4.

5.

6.

7.

8.

9.

10.

May 7

 List 10 favorite places that you have visited

1.

2.

3.

4.

5.

6.

7.

8.

9.

10.

May 8

 List 10 people who have positively influenced you

1.

2.

3.

4.

5.

6.

7.

8.

9.

10.

May 9

 List 10 things that set you apart from everyone else

1.

2.

3.

4.

5.

6.

7.

8.

9.

10.

May 10

List 10 subjects that you would like to learn more about

1.

2.

3.

4.

5.

6.

7.

8.

9.

10.

May 11

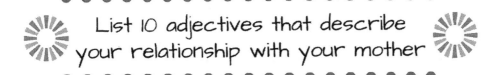

List 10 adjectives that describe your relationship with your mother

1.

2.

3.

4.

5.

6.

7.

8.

9.

10.

May 12

List 10 things that happened this past week for which you are grateful

1.

2.

3.

4.

5.

6.

7.

8.

9.

10.

May 13

 List 10 things that you are looking forward to this week

1.

2.

3.

4.

5.

6.

7.

8.

9.

10.

May 14

 List 10 social/humanitarian causes that you care deeply about

1.

2.

3.

4.

5.

6.

7.

8.

9.

10.

May 15

List 10 simple things that you can do right now to add more joy to your life

1.

2.

3.

4.

5.

6.

7.

8.

9.

10.

May 16

 List 10 compliments that you regularly receive

1.

2.

3.

4.

5.

6.

7.

8.

9.

10.

May 17

 List 10 habits that you would like to change

1.

2.

3.

4.

5.

6.

7.

8.

9.

10.

May 18

 List your 10 biggest time wasters

1.

2.

3.

4.

5.

6.

7.

8.

9.

10.

May 19

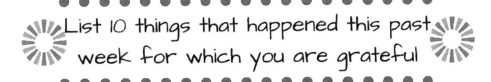
List 10 things that happened this past week for which you are grateful

1.

2.

3.

4.

5.

6.

7.

8.

9.

10.

May 20

 List 10 things that you are looking forward to this week

1.

2.

3.

4.

5.

6.

7.

8.

9.

10.

May 21

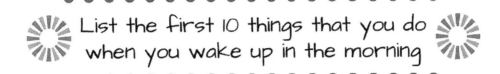
List the first 10 things that you do when you wake up in the morning

1.

2.

3.

4.

5.

6.

7.

8.

9.

10.

May 22

List the last 10 things you do before going to sleep at night

1.

2.

3.

4.

5.

6.

7.

8.

9.

10.

May 23

 List 10 great decisions that you've made in your life

1.

2.

3.

4.

5.

6.

7.

8.

9.

10.

May 24

List 10 favorite physical attributes that you possess

1.

2.

3.

4.

5.

6.

7.

8.

9.

10.

May 25

 List the 10 technological advances that you enjoy the most

1.

2.

3.

4.

5.

6.

7.

8.

9.

10.

May 26

List 10 things that happened this past week for which you are grateful

1.

2.

3.

4.

5.

6.

7.

8.

9.

10.

May 27

 List 10 things that you are looking forward to this week

1.

2.

3.

4.

5.

6.

7.

8.

9.

10.

May 28

List 10 songs that would be on your ideal workout playlist

1.

2.

3.

4.

5.

6.

7.

8.

9.

10.

May 29

List 10 things that you would like to do differently tomorrow than you did today

1.

2.

3.

4.

5.

6.

7.

8.

9.

10.

May 30

 List 10 things that prevent you from experiencing stillness

1.

2.

3.

4.

5.

6.

7.

8.

9.

10.

May 31

 List 10 highlights of the past month

1.

2.

3.

4.

5.

6.

7.

8.

9.

10.

June 1

 List 10 things that you are looking forward to this month

1.

2.

3.

4.

5.

6.

7.

8.

9.

10.

June 2

List 10 things that happened this past week for which you are grateful

1.

2.

3.

4.

5.

6.

7.

8.

9.

10.

June 3

 List 10 things that you are looking forward to this week

1.

2.

3.

4.

5.

6.

7.

8.

9.

10.

June 4

List 10 accomplishments that make you proud

1.

2.

3.

4.

5.

6.

7.

8.

9.

10.

June 5

 List 10 things that people would be surprised to learn about you

1.

2.

3.

4.

5.

6.

7.

8.

9.

10.

June 6

 List 10 great ideas that you have right now

1.

2.

3.

4.

5.

6.

7.

8.

9.

10.

June 7

List 10 things that you never want to do/experience again

1.

2.

3.

4.

5.

6.

7.

8.

9.

10.

June 8

List your 10 favorite guilty pleasures

1.

2.

3.

4.

5.

6.

7.

8.

9.

10.

June 9

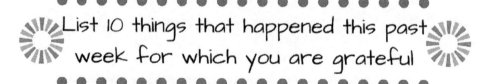

List 10 things that happened this past week for which you are grateful

1.

2.

3.

4.

5.

6.

7.

8.

9.

10.

June 10

 List 10 things that you are looking forward to this week

1.

2.

3.

4.

5.

6.

7.

8.

9.

10.

June 11

 List 10 things that you tend to do when you are upset

1.

2.

3.

4.

5.

6.

7.

8.

9.

10.

June 12

 List the 10 people whom you love most in the world

1.

2.

3.

4.

5.

6.

7.

8.

9.

10.

June 13

 List 10 highlights from the past six months

1.

2.

3.

4.

5.

6.

7.

8.

9.

10.

June 14

List 10 goals that you have for the next six months

1.

2.

3.

4.

5.

6.

7.

8.

9.

10.

June 15

 List 10 adjectives that describe your relationship with your father

1.

2.

3.

4.

5.

6.

7.

8.

9.

10.

June 16

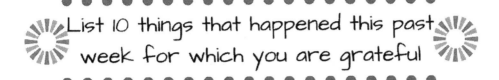
List 10 things that happened this past week for which you are grateful

1.

2.

3.

4.

5.

6.

7.

8.

9.

10.

June 17

 List 10 things that you are looking forward to this week

1.

2.

3.

4.

5.

6.

7.

8.

9.

10.

June 18

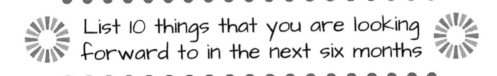
List 10 things that you are looking forward to in the next six months

1.

2.

3.

4.

5.

6.

7.

8.

9.

10.

June 19

 List 10 limiting beliefs that are holding you back

1.

2.

3.

4.

5.

6.

7.

8.

9.

10.

June 20

List 10 empowering beliefs that can replace your limiting beliefs

1.

2.

3.

4.

5.

6.

7.

8.

9.

10.

June 21

 List 10 opportunities that you are currently looking for

1.

2.

3.

4.

5.

6.

7.

8.

9.

10.

June 22

 List 10 ways in which you can change someone's life for the better

1.

2.

3.

4.

5.

6.

7.

8.

9.

10.

June 23

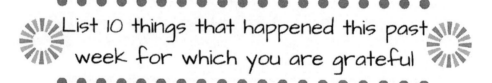

List 10 things that happened this past week for which you are grateful

1.

2.

3.

4.

5.

6.

7.

8.

9.

10.

June 24

 List 10 things that you are looking forward to this week

1.

2.

3.

4.

5.

6.

7.

8.

9.

10.

June 25

List 10 items that you would insist on having if you had to spend a year alone on a deserted island

1.

2.

3.

4.

5.

6.

7.

8.

9.

10.

June 26

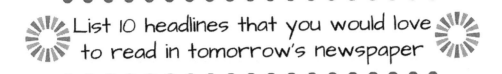
List 10 headlines that you would love to read in tomorrow's newspaper

1.

2.

3.

4.

5.

6.

7.

8.

9.

10.

June 27

 List the last 10 things that you truly celebrated

1.

2.

3.

4.

5.

6.

7.

8.

9.

10.

June 28

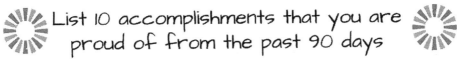
List 10 accomplishments that you are proud of from the past 90 days

1.

2.

3.

4.

5.

6.

7.

8.

9.

10.

June 29

 List 10 goals that you have for the next 90 days

1.

2.

3.

4.

5.

6.

7.

8.

9.

10.

June 30

 List 10 highlights of the past month

1.

2.

3.

4.

5.

6.

7.

8.

9.

10.

July 1

 List 10 things that you are looking forward to this week

1.

2.

3.

4.

5.

6.

7.

8.

9.

10.

July 2

 List 10 things that you are looking forward to this month

1.

2.

3.

4.

5.

6.

7.

8.

9.

10.

July 3

 List 10 things that you love about summer

1.

2.

3.

4.

5.

6.

7.

8.

9.

10.

July 4

 List 10 personal freedoms that you most enjoy

1.

2.

3.

4.

5.

6.

7.

8.

9.

10.

July 5

 List 10 things that you love about being your gender

1.

2.

3.

4.

5.

6.

7.

8.

9.

10.

July 6

List 10 songs that would be on your ideal "party" playlist

1.

2.

3.

4.

5.

6.

7.

8.

9.

10.

July 7

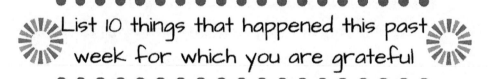
List 10 things that happened this past week for which you are grateful

1.

2.

3.

4.

5.

6.

7.

8.

9.

10.

July 8

 List 10 things that you are looking forward to this week

1.

2.

3.

4.

5.

6.

7.

8.

9.

10.

July 9

 List 10 activities that you enjoy doing with your friends

1. Going to the OCEAN
2. MOVIE NIGHTS
3. GOING THE POOL
4. GOING TO FOOD
5. GOING TO THE LAKE
6. SKATEBOARDING
7. AMUSMENT PARKS
8.
9.
10.

July 10

List 10 activities that you enjoy doing with your spouse/partner

1.

2.

3.

4.

5.

6.

7.

8.

9.

10.

July 11

List 10 activities that you enjoy doing with your family

1.

2.

3.

4.

5.

6.

7.

8.

9.

10.

July 12

 List 10 activities that you enjoy doing all by yourself

1.

2.

3.

4.

5.

6.

7.

8.

9.

10.

July 13

List 10 beliefs that you used to have but no longer do

1.

2.

3.

4.

5.

6.

7.

8.

9.

10.

July 14

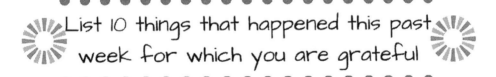
List 10 things that happened this past week for which you are grateful

1.

2.

3.

4.

5.

6.

7.

8.

9.

10.

July 15

List 10 things that you are looking forward to this week

1.

2.

3.

4.

5.

6.

7.

8.

9.

10.

July 16

List 10 things that you believe should be included in wedding vows

1.

2.

3.

4.

5.

6.

7.

8.

9.

10.

July 17

List 10 things that you would do differently if you weren't worried about other people's opinions

1.

2.

3.

4.

5.

6.

7.

8.

9.

10.

July 18

 List 10 patterns that tend to repeat in your life

1.

2.

3.

4.

5.

6.

7.

8.

9.

10.

July 19

List 10 ways in which you could be kinder to yourself

1.

2.

3.

4.

5.

6.

7.

8.

9.

10.

July 20

 List 10 thoughts that you have about aging

1.

2.

3.

4.

5.

6.

7.

8.

9.

10.

July 21

List 10 things that happened this past week for which you are grateful

1.

2.

3.

4.

5.

6.

7.

8.

9.

10.

July 22

 List 10 things that you are looking forward to this week

1.

2.

3.

4.

5.

6.

7.

8.

9.

10.

July 23

List 10 things that you would do if you suddenly had ten million dollars

1.

2.

3.

4.

5.

6.

7.

8.

9.

10.

July 24

List Your 10 favorite daily activities

1.

2.

3.

4.

5.

6.

7.

8.

9.

10.

July 25

 List 10 mind-blowing experiences that you've had but can't explain

1.

2.

3.

4.

5.

6.

7.

8.

9.

10.

July 26

 List 10 articles of clothing that would be in your dream closet

1.

2.

3.

4.

5.

6.

7.

8.

9.

10.

July 27

List 10 words that describe your relationship with your significant other

1.

2.

3.

4.

5.

6.

7.

8.

9.

10.

July 28

List 10 things that happened this past week for which you are grateful

1.

2.

3.

4.

5.

6.

7.

8.

9.

10.

July 29

 List 10 things that you are looking forward to this week

1.

2.

3.

4.

5.

6.

7.

8.

9.

10.

July 30

 List 10 superstitions that you believe

1.

2.

3.

4.

5.

6.

7.

8.

9.

10.

July 31

List 10 highlights of the past month

1.

2.

3.

4.

5.

6.

7.

8.

9.

10.

August 1

 List 10 things that you are looking forward to this month

1.

2.

3.

4.

5.

6.

7.

8.

9.

10.

August 2

 List 10 valuable lessons that you have learned in life

1.

2.

3.

4.

5.

6.

7.

8.

9.

10.

August 3

 List 10 personal traits that you try to hide from others

1.

2.

3.

4.

5.

6.

7.

8.

9.

10.

August 4

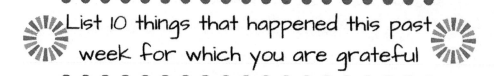
List 10 things that happened this past week for which you are grateful

1.

2.

3.

4.

5.

6.

7.

8.

9.

10.

August 5

 List 10 things that you are looking forward to this week

1.

2.

3.

4.

5.

6.

7.

8.

9.

10.

August 6

List your 10 biggest money wasters

1.

2.

3.

4.

5.

6.

7.

8.

9.

10.

August 7

List 10 thoughts that you hope other people have about you

1.

2.

3.

4.

5.

6.

7.

8.

9.

10.

August 8

List 10 things that you are currently doing to take care of your physical health

1.

2.

3.

4.

5.

6.

7.

8.

9.

10.

August 9

List 10 things that you are currently doing to take care of your emotional health

1.

2.

3.

4.

5.

6.

7.

8.

9.

10.

August 10

List 10 people who have already accomplished goals similar to the ones that you want to accomplish

1.

2.

3.

4.

5.

6.

7.

8.

9.

10.

August 11

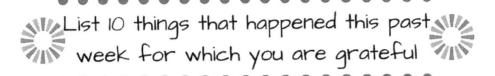
List 10 things that happened this past week for which you are grateful

1.

2.

3.

4.

5.

6.

7.

8.

9.

10.

August 12

List 10 things that you are looking forward to this week

1.

2.

3.

4.

5.

6.

7.

8.

9.

10.

August 13

List 10 things that you regularly say to yourself

1.

2.

3.

4.

5.

6.

7.

8.

9.

10.

August 14

 List 10 fictional characters that you wish were real

1.

2.

3.

4.

5.

6.

7.

8.

9.

10.

August 15

 List 10 ways in which you can connect with your Higher Power

1.

2.

3.

4.

5.

6.

7.

8.

9.

10.

August 16

 List your 10 biggest regrets in life, so far

1.

2.

3.

4.

5.

6.

7.

8.

9.

10.

August 17

List 10 ways that you add value to your work place

1.

2.

3.

4.

5.

6.

7.

8.

9.

10.

August 18

List 10 things that happened this past week for which you are grateful

1.

2.

3.

4.

5.

6.

7.

8.

9.

10.

August 19

List 10 things that you are looking forward to this week

1.

2.

3.

4.

5.

6.

7.

8.

9.

10.

August 20

 List 10 challenges that you have overcome in life

1.

2.

3.

4.

5.

6.

7.

8.

9.

10.

August 21

List 10 things that you hope to accomplish in the next five years

1.

2.

3.

4.

5.

6.

7.

8.

9.

10.

August 22

 List 10 things that you hope to accomplish in the next ten years

1.

2.

3.

4.

5.

6.

7.

8.

9.

10.

August 23

 List 10 things that you hope to accomplish in your lifetime

1.

2.

3.

4.

5.

6.

7.

8.

9.

10.

August 24

 List 10 things that you would fight to the death for

1.

2.

3.

4.

5.

6.

7.

8.

9.

10.

August 25

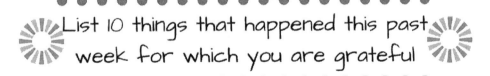
List 10 things that happened this past week for which you are grateful

1.

2.

3.

4.

5.

6.

7.

8.

9.

10.

August 26

List 10 things that you are looking forward to this week

1.

2.

3.

4.

5.

6.

7.

8.

9.

10.

August 27

List 10 songs that make up your ideal "I want to punch someone in the face" playlist

1.

2.

3.

4.

5.

6.

7.

8.

9.

10.

August 28

 List 10 things that you love about your current home

1.

2.

3.

4.

5.

6.

7.

8.

9.

10.

August 29

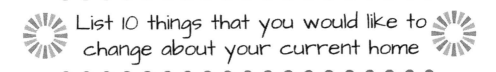
List 10 things that you would like to change about your current home

1.

2.

3.

4.

5.

6.

7.

8.

9.

10.

August 30

 List 10 things that fascinate you

1.

2.

3.

4.

5.

6.

7.

8.

9.

10.

August 31

 List 10 highlights of the past month

1.

2.

3.

4.

5.

6.

7.

8.

9.

10.

September 1

List 10 things that happened this past week for which you are grateful

1.

2.

3.

4.

5.

6.

7.

8.

9.

10.

September 2

 List 10 things that you are looking forward to this week

1.

2.

3.

4.

5.

6.

7.

8.

9.

10.

September 3

List 10 things that you are looking forward to this month

1.

2.

3.

4.

5.

6.

7.

8.

9.

10.

September 4

 List 10 things that always put a smile on your face

1.

2.

3.

4.

5.

6.

7.

8.

9.

10.

September 5

 List 10 things that fire you up

1.

2.

3.

4.

5.

6.

7.

8.

9.

10.

September 6

 List 10 things that chill you out

1.

2.

3.

4.

5.

6.

7.

8.

9.

10.

September 7

List 10 areas of your life in which your are settling for less than you deserve

1.

2.

3.

4.

5.

6.

7.

8.

9.

10.

September 8

List 10 things that happened this past week for which you are grateful

1.

2.

3.

4.

5.

6.

7.

8.

9.

10.

September 9

List 10 things that you are looking forward to this week

1.

2.

3.

4.

5.

6.

7.

8.

9.

10.

September 10

 List 10 thoughts that you have regarding the current state of world affairs

1.

2.

3.

4.

5.

6.

7.

8.

9.

10.

September 11

 List 10 lies that you tell yourself

1.

2.

3.

4.

5.

6.

7.

8.

9.

10.

September 12

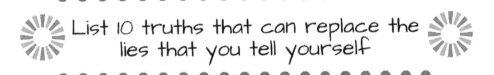

List 10 truths that can replace the lies that you tell yourself

1.

2.

3.

4.

5.

6.

7.

8.

9.

10.

September 13

 List your 10 favorite outdoor activites

1.

2.

3.

4.

5.

6.

7.

8.

9.

10.

September 14

List your 10 favorite indoor activites

1.

2.

3.

4.

5.

6.

7.

8.

9.

10.

September 15

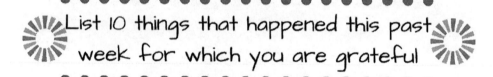
List 10 things that happened this past week for which you are grateful

1.

2.

3.

4.

5.

6.

7.

8.

9.

10.

September 16

 List 10 things that you are looking forward to this week

1.

2.

3.

4.

5.

6.

7.

8.

9.

10.

September 17

 List your 10 most consistent worries

1.

2.

3.

4.

5.

6.

7.

8.

9.

10.

September 18

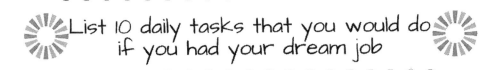

1.

2.

3.

4.

5.

6.

7.

8.

9.

10.

September 19

 List 10 ways that you add value to your family

1.

2.

3.

4.

5.

6.

7.

8.

9.

10.

September 20

 List 10 things that you hope to purchase in the next year

1.

2.

3.

4.

5.

6.

7.

8.

9.

10.

September 21

 List 10 risks that you have taken in life

1.

2.

3.

4.

5.

6.

7.

8.

9.

10.

September 22

List 10 things that happened this past week for which you are grateful

1.

2.

3.

4.

5.

6.

7.

8.

9.

10.

September 23

 List 10 things that you are looking forward to this week

1.

2.

3.

4.

5.

6.

7.

8.

9.

10.

September 24

List 10 things that make you feel whole

1.

2.

3.

4.

5.

6.

7.

8.

9.

10.

September 25

 List 10 things that make you feel fractured

1.

2.

3.

4.

5.

6.

7.

8.

9.

10.

September 26

List 10 accomplishments that you are proud of from the past 90 days

1.

2.

3.

4.

5.

6.

7.

8.

9.

10.

September 27

 List 10 goals that you have for the next 90 days

1.

2.

3.

4.

5.

6.

7.

8.

9.

10.

September 28

List 10 highlights of the past month

1.

2.

3.

4.

5.

6.

7.

8.

9.

10.

September 29

List 10 things that happened this past week for which you are grateful

1.

2.

3.

4.

5.

6.

7.

8.

9.

10.

September 30

 List 10 things that you are looking forward to this week

1.

2.

3.

4.

5.

6.

7.

8.

9.

10.

October 1

List 10 things that you are looking forward to this month

1.

2.

3.

4.

5.

6.

7.

8.

9.

10.

October 2

List 10 miracles that you have witnessed

1.

2.

3.

4.

5.

6.

7.

8.

9.

10.

October 3

 List your 10 favorite things about autumn

1.

2.

3.

4.

5.

6.

7.

8.

9.

10.

October 4

 List your 10 favorite quotes

1.

2.

3.

4.

5.

6.

7.

8.

9.

10.

October 5

 List 10 things that energize you

1.

2.

3.

4.

5.

6.

7.

8.

9.

10.

October 6

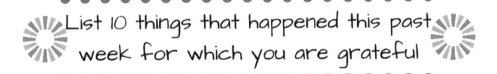
List 10 things that happened this past week for which you are grateful

1.

2.

3.

4.

5.

6.

7.

8.

9.

10.

October 7

 List 10 things that you are looking forward to this week

1.

2.

3.

4.

5.

6.

7.

8.

9.

10.

October 8

 List 10 things that you are busy with today

1.

2.

3.

4.

5.

6.

7.

8.

9.

10.

October 9

 List 10 things that you love about fall

1.

2.

3.

4.

5.

6.

7.

8.

9.

10.

October 10

 List the 10 biggest contributions that you bring to the world

1.

2.

3.

4.

5.

6.

7.

8.

9.

10.

October 11

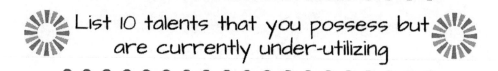

List 10 talents that you possess but are currently under-utilizing

1.

2.

3.

4.

5.

6.

7.

8.

9.

10.

October 12

 List 10 attributes of your dream job

1.

2.

3.

4.

5.

6.

7.

8.

9.

10.

October 13

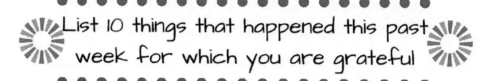

List 10 things that happened this past week for which you are grateful

1.

2.

3.

4.

5.

6.

7.

8.

9.

10.

October 14

 List 10 things that you are looking forward to this week

1.

2.

3.

4.

5.

6.

7.

8.

9.

10.

October 15

 List 10 things that you feel guilty about

1.

2.

3.

4.

5.

6.

7.

8.

9.

10.

October 16

 List 10 people who love you

1.

2.

3.

4.

5.

6.

7.

8.

9.

10.

October 17

 List 10 things that you do when you are happy

1.

2.

3.

4.

5.

6.

7.

8.

9.

10.

October 18

 List 10 things that drain you of your energy

1.

2.

3.

4.

5.

6.

7.

8.

9.

10.

October 19

 List 10 good habits that you'd like to cultivate in your life

1.

2.

3.

4.

5.

6.

7.

8.

9.

10.

October 20

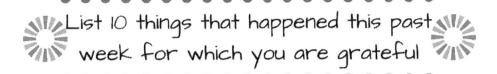
List 10 things that happened this past week for which you are grateful

1.

2.

3.

4.

5.

6.

7.

8.

9.

10.

October 21

List 10 things that you are looking forward to this week

1.

2.

3.

4.

5.

6.

7.

8.

9.

10.

October 22

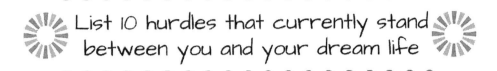
List 10 hurdles that currently stand between you and your dream life

1.

2.

3.

4.

5.

6.

7.

8.

9.

10.

October 23

 List 10 things that are currently working well in your life

1.

2.

3.

4.

5.

6.

7.

8.

9.

10.

October 24

 List 10 things that you are excited about right now

1.

2.

3.

4.

5.

6.

7.

8.

9.

10.

October 25

 List the 10 people that you spend the most time with

1. Mom
2. Naya
3. Lily
4. Grace
5. Heidi
6. Chloe
7. Ken
8. Keira
9. Mif
10. Abby

October 26

List 10 things that you absolutely will not tolerate in your life

1.

2.

3.

4.

5.

6.

7.

8.

9.

10.

October 27

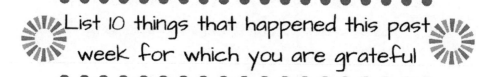

List 10 things that happened this past week for which you are grateful

1.

2.

3.

4.

5.

6.

7.

8.

9.

10.

October 28

 List 10 things that you are looking forward to this week

1.

2.

3.

4.

5.

6.

7.

8.

9.

10.

October 29

 List 10 things that you are passionate about

1.

2.

3.

4.

5.

6.

7.

8.

9.

10.

October 30

 List 10 highlights of the past month

1.

2.

3.

4.

5.

6.

7.

8.

9.

10.

October 31

 List your 10 biggest fears

1.

2.

3.

4.

5.

6.

7.

8.

9.

10.

November 1

List 10 things that you are looking forward to this month

1.

2.

3.

4.

5.

6.

7.

8.

9.

10.

November 2

List 10 ways in which you can add meaning to your life

1.

2.

3.

4.

5.

6.

7.

8.

9.

10.

November 3

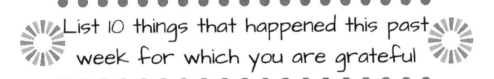
List 10 things that happened this past week for which you are grateful

1.

2.

3.

4.

5.

6.

7.

8.

9.

10.

November 4

 List 10 things that you are looking forward to this week

1.

2.

3.

4.

5.

6.

7.

8.

9.

10.

November 5

 List the 10 biggest stressors currently in your life

1.

2.

3.

4.

5.

6.

7.

8.

9.

10.

November 6

List 10 things that you would regret not having done, if the world ended tomorrow

1.

2.

3.

4.

5.

6.

7.

8.

9.

10.

November 7

List 10 things that give you a sense of "home"

1.

2.

3.

4.

5.

6.

7.

8.

9.

10.

November 8

 List 10 date ideas that sound fun to you

1.

2.

3.

4.

5.

6.

7.

8.

9.

10.

November 9

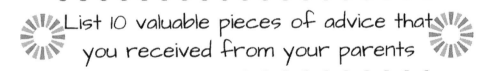

List 10 valuable pieces of advice that you received from your parents

1.

2.

3.

4.

5.

6.

7.

8.

9.

10.

November 10

List 10 things that happened this past week for which you are grateful

1.

2.

3.

4.

5.

6.

7.

8.

9.

10.

November 11

 List 10 things that you are looking forward to this week

1.

2.

3.

4.

5.

6.

7.

8.

9.

10.

November 12

 List 10 things that always make you laugh

1.

2.

3.

4.

5.

6.

7.

8.

9.

10.

November 13

List 10 things that you need in order to feel truly content

1.

2.

3.

4.

5.

6.

7.

8.

9.

10.

November 14

List the 10 biggest turning points, thus far, in your life

1. moving from Marin
2.
3.
4.
5.
6.
7.
8.
9.
10.

November 15

List 10 things that you are currently trying to heal (physically and emotionally) in your life

1. Riding
2.
3.
4.
5.
6.
7.
8.
9.
10.

November 16

List 10 ways in which you add value in your friendships

1.

2.

3.

4.

5.

6.

7.

8.

9.

10.

November 17

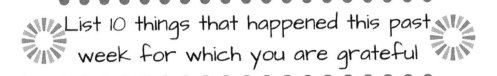

1.

2.

3.

4.

5.

6.

7.

8.

9.

10.

November 18

 List 10 things that you are looking forward to this week

1.

2.

3.

4.

5.

6.

7.

8.

9.

10.

November 19

 List 10 things that you can do right now that will move you closer to your goals

1.

2.

3.

4.

5.

6.

7.

8.

9.

10.

November 20

 List 10 flavors that you love

1.

2.

3.

4.

5.

6.

7.

8.

9.

10.

November 21

 List 10 things that you are most thankful for today

1.

2.

3.

4.

5.

6.

7.

8.

9.

10.

November 22

 List 10 experiences that always leave you with a sense of awe

1.

2.

3.

4.

5.

6.

7.

8.

9.

10.

November 23

List your 10 current favorite songs on your playlist

1.

2.

3.

4.

5.

6.

7.

8.

9.

10.

November 24

List 10 things that happened this past week for which you are grateful

1.

2.

3.

4.

5.

6.

7.

8.

9.

10.

November 25

 List 10 things that you are looking forward to this week

1.

2.

3.

4.

5.

6.

7.

8.

9.

10.

November 26

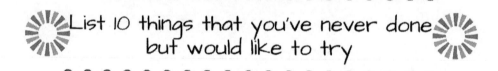

List 10 things that you've never done but would like to try

1.

2.

3.

4.

5.

6.

7.

8.

9.

10.

November 27

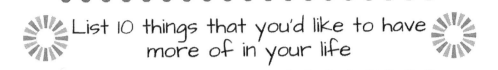

List 10 things that you'd like to have more of in your life

1.

2.

3.

4.

5.

6.

7.

8.

9.

10.

November 28

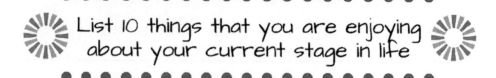

List 10 things that you are enjoying about your current stage in life

1.

2.

3.

4.

5.

6.

7.

8.

9.

10.

November 29

 List 10 not-so-great decisions that you've made in your life

1.

2.

3.

4.

5.

6.

7.

8.

9.

10.

November 30

 List 10 highlights of the past month

1.

2.

3.

4.

5.

6.

7.

8.

9.

10.

December 1

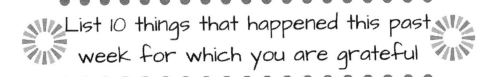

List 10 things that happened this past week for which you are grateful

1.

2.

3.

4.

5.

6.

7.

8.

9.

10.

December 2

List 10 things that you are looking forward to this week

1.

2.

3.

4.

5.

6.

7.

8.

9.

10.

December 3

List 10 things that you are looking forward to this month

1.

2.

3.

4.

5.

6.

7.

8.

9.

10.

December 4

List 10 things that you are avoiding or putting off in your life

1.

2.

3.

4.

5.

6.

7.

8.

9.

10.

December 5

 List 10 things that inspire you

1.

2.

3.

4.

5.

6.

7.

8.

9.

10.

December 6

List 10 attributes of your dream home

1.

2.

3.

4.

5.

6.

7.

8.

9.

10.

December 7

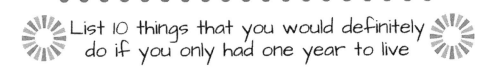

List 10 things that you would definitely do if you only had one year to live

1.

2.

3.

4.

5.

6.

7.

8.

9.

10.

December 8

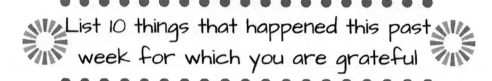
List 10 things that happened this past week for which you are grateful

1.

2.

3.

4.

5.

6.

7.

8.

9.

10.

December 9

 List 10 things that you are looking forward to this week

1.

2.

3.

4.

5.

6.

7.

8.

9.

10.

December 10

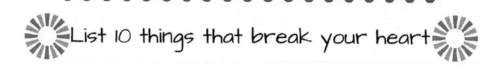

1.

2.

3.

4.

5.

6.

7.

8.

9.

10.

December 11

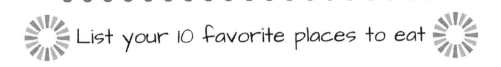
List your 10 favorite places to eat

1.

2.

3.

4.

5.

6.

7.

8.

9.

10.

December 12

 List your 10 deepest, darkest secrets

1.

2.

3.

4.

5.

6.

7.

8.

9.

10.

December 13

 List 10 people whom you need to forgive

1.

2.

3.

4.

5.

6.

7.

8.

9.

10.

December 14

 List 10 interesting things about yourself

1.

2.

3.

4.

5.

6.

7.

8.

9.

10.

December 15

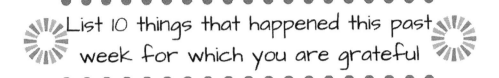
List 10 things that happened this past week for which you are grateful

1.

2.

3.

4.

5.

6.

7.

8.

9.

10.

December 16

 List 10 things that you are looking forward to this week

1.

2.

3.

4.

5.

6.

7.

8.

9.

10.

December 17

List 10 rules that you live your life in adherence to

1.

2.

3.

4.

5.

6.

7.

8.

9.

10.

December 18

 List 10 fears that you have successfully overcome

1.

2.

3.

4.

5.

6.

7.

8.

9.

10.

December 19

 List 10 things that you believe you were put upon this earth to do

1.

2.

3.

4.

5.

6.

7.

8.

9.

10.

December 20

List 10 things that you would like to be a part of the legacy you leave behind

1.

2.

3.

4.

5.

6.

7.

8.

9.

10.

December 21
List 10 things that need to happen in order for you to live your most fulfilled life

1.

2.

3.

4.

5.

6.

7.

8.

9.

10.

December 22

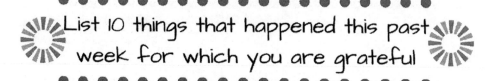
List 10 things that happened this past week for which you are grateful

1.

2.

3.

4.

5.

6.

7.

8.

9.

10.

December 23

 List 10 things that you are looking forward to this week

1.

2.

3.

4.

5.

6.

7.

8.

9.

10.

December 24

 List 10 gifts that you love to give

1.

2.

3.

4.

5.

6.

7.

8.

9.

10.

December 25

List your 10 favorite family traditions

1.

2.

3.

4.

5.

6.

7.

8.

9.

10.

December 26

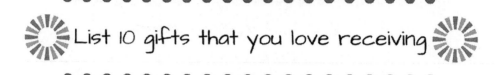

1.

2.

3.

4.

5.

6.

7.

8.

9.

10.

December 27

 List the 10 most special gifts that you've received in your lifetime

1.

2.

3.

4.

5.

6.

7.

8.

9.

10.

December 28

List 10 highlights of the past month

1.

2.

3.

4.

5.

6.

7.

8.

9.

10.

December 29

 List 10 valuable lessons that you've learned over the past year

1.

2.

3.

4.

5.

6.

7.

8.

9.

10.

December 30

 List 10 highlights of the past year

1.

2.

3.

4.

5.

6.

7.

8.

9.

10.

December 31

 List 10 things that you are looking forward to in the next year

1.

2.

3.

4.

5.

6.

7.

8.

9.

10.

Coming Soon

Forever FabYOUlous: Flaunting Your FAB in your 40's and Beyond

Finding FabYOUlous Workbook and Journal

Also by this Author

Finding FabYOUlous: A 'Self-Help with Sass' Guide to Finding, Celebrating and Capitalizing on the FabYOUlousness that Makes You, YOU

For updates on these publications *and* the latest information on FabYOUlous Life news and events, please visit www.FabYOUlousLife.com and subscribe to the mailing list.

Follow the Fab

@FabYOUlousLife   @FabYOUlous_Life   @FabYOUlousLife   @FabYOUlousLife

About the Author

From trainwreck to trainer, Melissa Venable has taken the ride, hit the bottom, done the work and risen from the ashes. She brings the agony *and* the inspiration from her experiences of wrestling with a life-threatening Anorexia Nervosa diagnosis and battling to escape an emotionally (and sometimes physically) abusive marriage; and delivers a message of hope, empowerment and love to women who long to rediscover and re-ignite their innate FabYOUlousness.

As a certified Life Coach, author and speaker, Melissa is the founder of the popular personal development website, FabYOUlousLife.com and has been featured on *Ewomen Network Radio* and in publications including *Mind + Body Magazine* and *Ladies Home Journal*. In 2015, she was honored as one of twelve "Colorado Women of Vision".

Melissa lives with her husband and three cats in northern Colorado at the base of the gorgeous Rocky Mountains. She has two young adult sons and a young adult step-daughter.

For information on working with Melissa or to schedule a speaking engagement, please visit the contact tab at www.FabYOUlousLife.com

● ●

Made in the USA
San Bernardino, CA
11 January 2019